OUR BODY

# Circulatory System

## Cheryl Jakab

Smart Apple Media

Smart Apple Media
2140 Howard Drive West
North Mankato
Minnesota 56003

First published in 2006 by
MACMILLAN EDUCATION AUSTRALIA PTY LTD
627 Chapel Street, South Yarra, Australia 3141

Visit our Web site at www.macmillan.com.au

Associated companies and representatives throughout the world.

Library of Congress Cataloging-in-Publication Data

Jakab, Cheryl.
    The circulatory system / Cheryl Jakab.
    p. cm. — (Our body)
    Includes index.
    ISBN-13: 978-1-58340-733-2
    1. Blood—Circulation—Juvenile literature. I. Title.

QP103.J35 2006
612.I—dc22                                              2005056803


Edited by Ruth Jelley
Text and cover design by Peter Shaw
Illustrations by Guy Holt, Jeff Lang (p. 4 (bottom), pp. 5–6, p. 18),
    and Ann Likhovetsky (p. 30)
Photo research by Legend Images

Printed in USA

**Acknowledgments**
The author and the publisher are grateful to the following for permission to reproduce copyright material:

Front cover photograph: Colored SEM/scanning electron micrograph of human blood showing red and white cells and platelets, courtesy of Photolibrary/National Cancer Institute/Science Photo Library.
Front cover illustration by Jeff Lang.

Wade Hughes/Lochman Transparencies, p. 21; Photolibrary/A.G.E. Fotostock, p. 22; Photolibrary/Science Photo Library, pp. 8, 12, 13, 20, 24, 26, 27, 29.

While every care has been taken to trace and acknowledge copyright, the publisher tenders their apologies for any accidental infringement where copyright has proved untraceable. Where the attempt has been unsuccessful, the publisher welcomes information that would redress the situation.

# Contents

**Glossary words**
When a word is printed in **bold**, you can look up its meaning in the Glossary on page 31.

# Amazing body structures

The human body is an amazing living thing. The structures of the body are divided into systems. Each system is made up of **cells**. Huge numbers of cells make up the **tissues** of the body systems. Each system performs a different, vital function. This series looks at six of the systems in the most familiar living thing to you—your body.

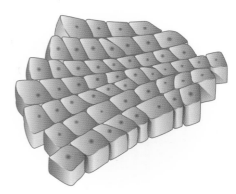

Cells make up tissues of the body systems.

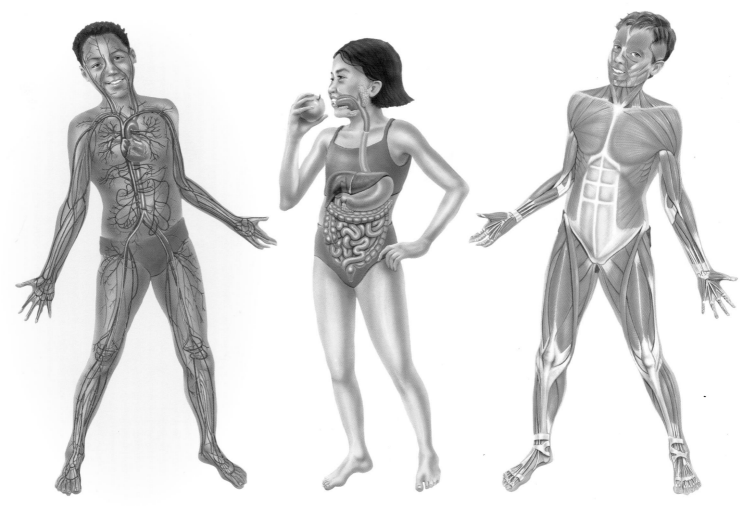

circulatory system        digestive system        muscular system

# The circulatory system

The circulatory system provides the body with gases and nutrients. How much do you know about your circulatory system?

- What is blood?
- What makes your blood look red?
- How long are the blood vessels in your body?
- What happens during a heart attack?

This book looks at the human circulatory system to answer these questions and more.

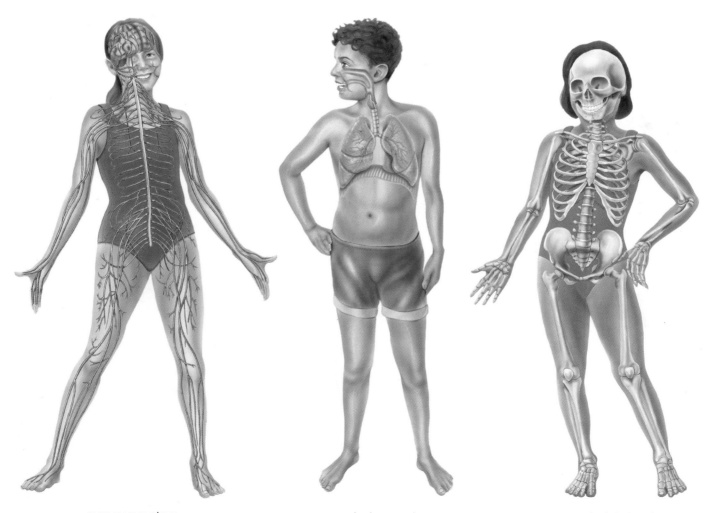

nervous system

respiratory system

skeletal system

# Parts of the circulatory system

The circulatory system is made up of the heart, **blood vessels**, and blood. Blood is contained within the heart and blood vessels (**arteries, veins,** and **capillaries**) at all times during circulation. In diagrams of the circulatory system, arteries are usually illustrated in red because most of them carry blood that is rich in **oxygen**. Veins are shown in blue because the blood in most veins is low in oxygen.

## You and your heart

Your heart is an organ that pumps blood around your body through the network of blood vessels. Long before scientists learned the function of the heart, people associated it with things such as love, loyalty, and courage.

**! FASCINATING FACT**
The circulatory system is also called the cardiovascular system. "Cardiovascular" comes from the Greek word "kardium" meaning heart and the Latin word "vasculum" meaning vessel.

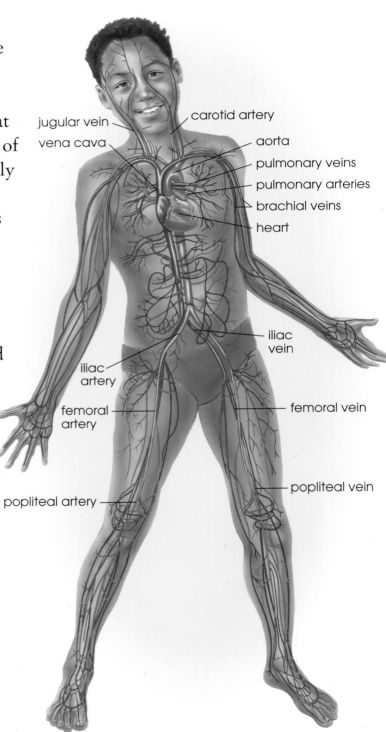

jugular vein
vena cava
carotid artery
aorta
pulmonary veins
pulmonary arteries
brachial veins
heart
iliac vein
iliac artery
femoral vein
femoral artery
popliteal vein
popliteal artery

Arteries take blood away from the heart.
Veins take blood back to the heart.

# The heart

The heart is protected by the ribs, which form a cage around the chest. If you could look inside your chest you would see a red lump about the size of a grapefruit with tubes coming out of it.

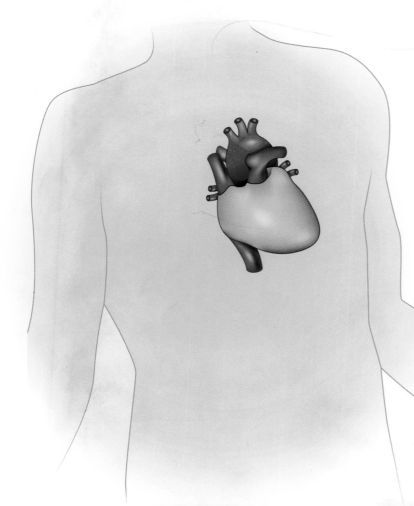

The heart lies just a little to the left of the middle of the chest.

## Blood vessels

Blood vessels form a branching network of channels like a tree. They transport blood from the heart to the rest of the body, and then back to the heart. There are about 93,210 miles (150,000 km) of blood vessels in the body.

## Blood

Blood is made up of cells in a watery liquid called **plasma**. Nearly half the volume of blood is made up of red blood cells, which give blood its red appearance.

**FASCINATING FACT**
The only living parts of the body without circulation are the lens and cornea in the eye. These parts must be clear to allow light to enter the eye, so they cannot have blood in them.

# Parts of the heart

The heart is an amazingly strong ball of muscle. It sits in a thin but strong bag called the pericardium. The pericardium is a smooth layer of connective tissue which supports and holds the heart. The outside of the heart has a rich network of **coronary arteries** and **coronary veins** to feed the heart muscle.

## Heart muscle

The heart is made of a special type of muscle called cardiac muscle. This muscle can work constantly without getting tired or needing a rest, and without you even being aware of it.

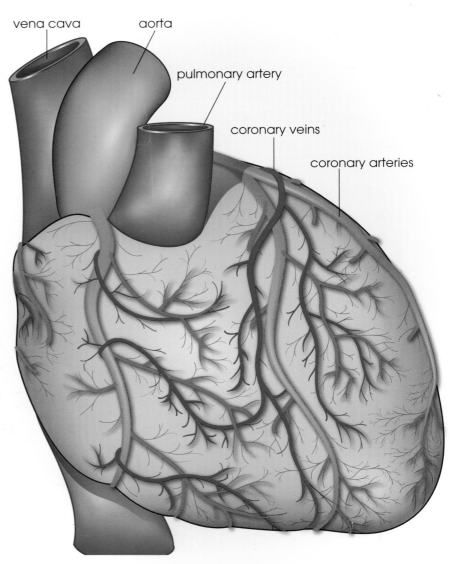

vena cava    aorta

pulmonary artery

coronary veins

coronary arteries

The heart is a ball of cardiac muscle which has a rich supply of blood.

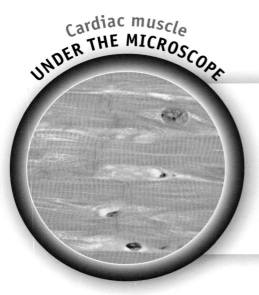

Cardiac muscle
UNDER THE MICROSCOPE

Cardiac muscle cells are closely connected to each other. Intercalated discs (the small vertical pink lines) allow fast communication between the cells of the heart muscle.

## Chambers of the heart

Inside the heart there are four spaces, or chambers. The upper and lower chambers are very different to each other. The two upper chambers, the **atria**, are small compared with the lower chambers, the **ventricles**. Atria have thin walls of muscle compared with the thick walls of the ventricles. There is a division down the middle of the heart, called the septum. The septum divides the heart into two sides, right and left. Each side is made up of one atrium and one ventricle.

**TRY THIS**

Look at a heart
Get the heart of a mammal, such as an ox or sheep, from a butcher. Look at the muscle, chambers, and valves of the heart.

## Valves in the heart

Valves are like taps which control the flow of blood in the heart. There are valves in the arteries that take blood out of the heart. There is also a valve between each atrium and ventricle.

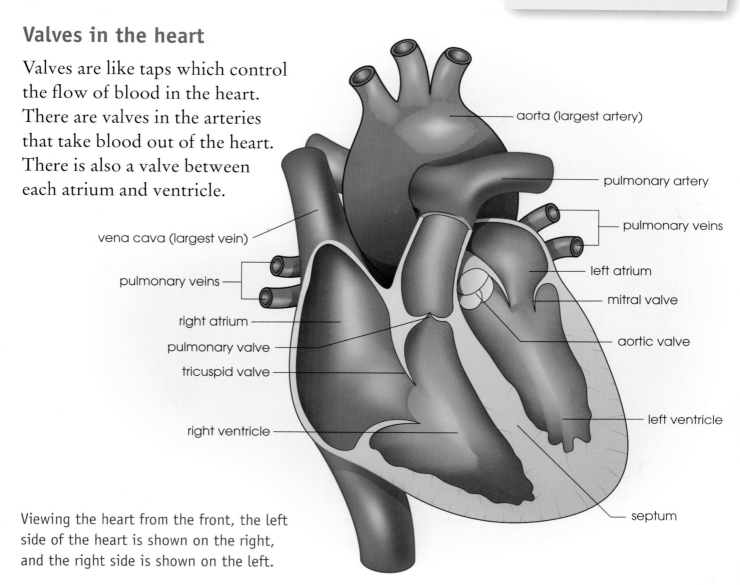

- aorta (largest artery)
- pulmonary artery
- pulmonary veins
- left atrium
- mitral valve
- aortic valve
- left ventricle
- septum
- vena cava (largest vein)
- pulmonary veins
- right atrium
- pulmonary valve
- tricuspid valve
- right ventricle

Viewing the heart from the front, the left side of the heart is shown on the right, and the right side is shown on the left.

# Differences in blood vessels

The different blood vessels of the body have different structures. Arteries have thick muscular walls to help push the blood from the heart to the rest of the body. Arteries branch out into smaller and smaller channels until they join the capillaries. The capillaries then connect to the smallest veins, which become larger and larger until they link back to the heart. Veins have thinner walls than arteries, as they do not have to be as strong as the arteries.

**FASCINATING FACT**
If you could lay out all the blood vessels in a body end-to-end they would go around Earth's equator at least two and a half times.

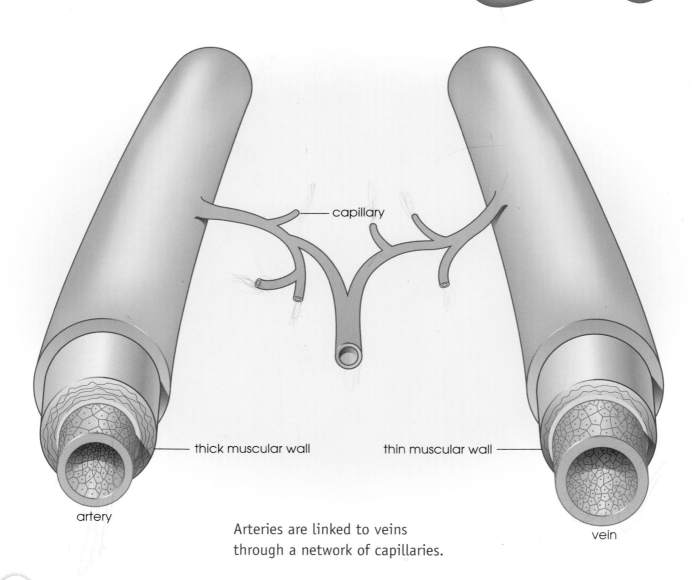

capillary

thick muscular wall

thin muscular wall

artery

vein

Arteries are linked to veins through a network of capillaries.

# The blood vessel network

The blood vessels form a network that extends to all parts of the body. The blood vessels leading in and out of the heart are the largest vessels. As the vessels spread throughout the body, they branch into smaller and smaller channels.

The major blood vessels have their own names. The aorta is the largest artery and the vena cava is the largest vein. The smallest arteries, called arterioles, divide into capillaries. The walls of the capillaries are just one cell thick. Capillaries connect to the smallest veins, called venules.

**FASCINATING FACT**
The ancient Greeks thought that arteries transported air, not blood. An English doctor, William Harvey (1578–1657), was the first to prove that blood circulated through a system of vessels.

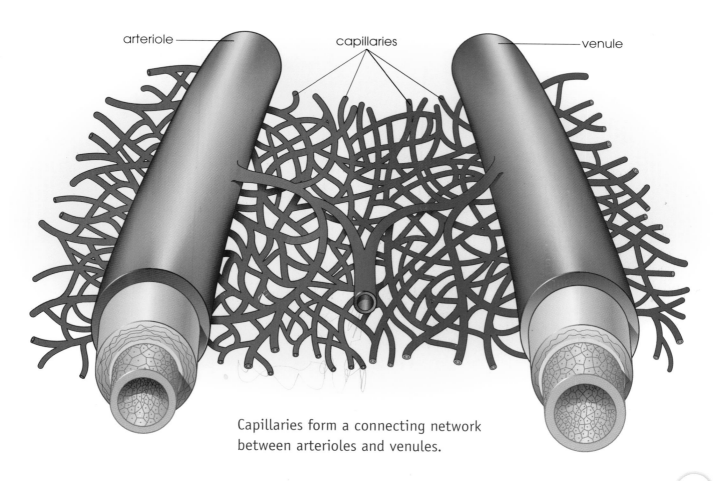

Capillaries form a connecting network between arterioles and venules.

# Parts of blood

Blood is made up of blood cells and plasma. Plasma is what makes the blood liquid. It is mostly water with a small amount of sugars and calcium and other substances dissolved in it. Less than half of the blood consists of blood cells and the rest is plasma.

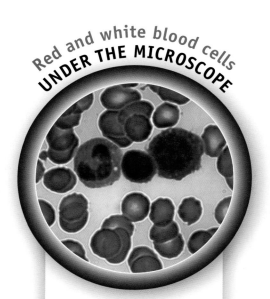

## Red and white blood cells UNDER THE MICROSCOPE

Here, three white blood cells (stained purple) can be seen with red blood cells. The dark patch inside the white blood cell is the nucleus, the cell's control center. Red blood cells do not have a nucleus.

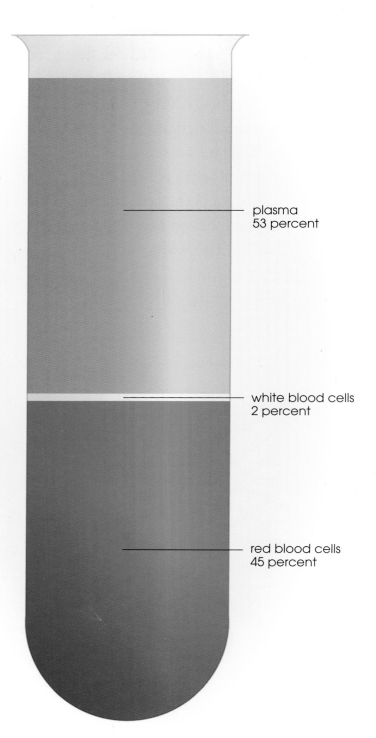

plasma
53 percent

white blood cells
2 percent

red blood cells
45 percent

Blood cells and plasma separate when a sample of blood is kept in a test tube.

# Red blood cells

Red blood cells make up most of the cells in blood. Red blood cells contain a substance called **hemoglobin**, which makes them red in color. Red blood cells are produced in the **bone marrow** and are released into the bloodstream when they are mature. As they age and become damaged, they are removed from the blood by an organ called the spleen.

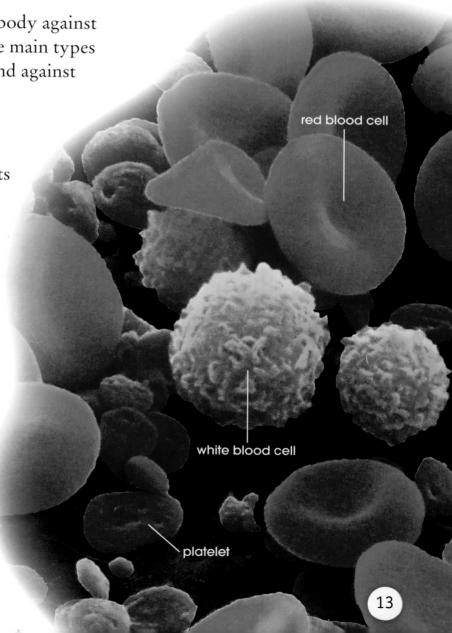

red blood cell

white blood cell

platelet

# White blood cells

White blood cells help to defend the body against infections and disease. There are three main types of white blood cells, which each defend against different types of diseases.

## Platelets

Platelets are small blood cell fragments which cause blood to **clot**.

## Blood cell life

Different types of blood cells have different life spans.

| Type of cell | Life span |
|---|---|
| red blood cells | 3–4 months |
| white blood cells | 7–14 days |
| platelets | 8–10 days |

Red blood cells are "biconcave discs" which are thin in the middle and have thick edges.

# Circulation

The circulatory system circulates food, oxygen, and other substances in the blood to all the body parts.

## Transfer of gases and nutrients

Gases and nutrients are transferred from blood to tissues through the capillary walls. Capillaries spread throughout the body so that all body parts can take part in this transfer. **Wastes** are transferred from the tissues to the blood so they can be removed from the body.

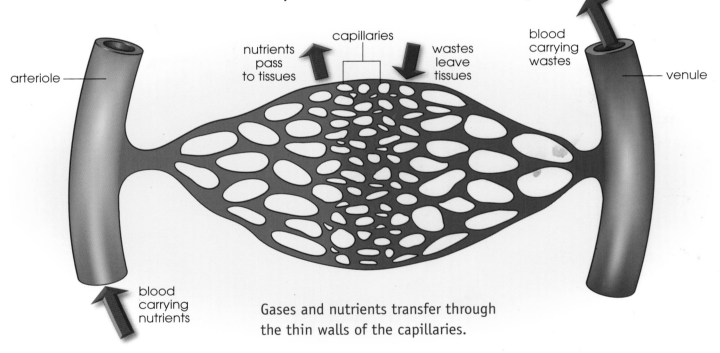

Gases and nutrients transfer through the thin walls of the capillaries.

## The heart and blood pressure

As the heart pushes blood through the network of vessels in the body, it causes a wave of pressure. This pressure inside the vessels is important for blood to flow through to all body parts. The left ventricle pushes the blood to all parts of the body. It has the thickest, strongest muscle of the heart which enables it to do this.

# Figure eight

Blood flows around the body in a pattern like a figure eight. Blood carrying oxygen flows from the lungs to the heart and is then pumped out to the rest of the body. The blood exchanges nutrients (oxygen) for wastes (carbon dioxide) in the body tissues and flows back to the heart. The blood carrying carbon dioxide is then pumped to the lungs where it releases carbon dioxide molecules and picks up oxygen molecules.

## Double pump

The heart is like a double pump because it pumps blood in two different directions at once. The right side of the heart pumps blood to the lungs to pick up oxygen. The left side of the heart pumps blood to the rest of the body to deliver the oxygen.

## TRY THIS

### Feel your pulse

Place three fingers flat over the inside of your wrist. Move them around until you feel a soft beat.

This is your **pulse**. It is the change of pressure in the blood moving through your blood vessels.

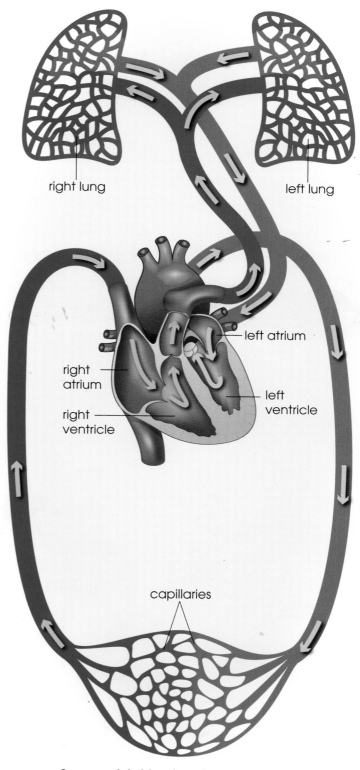

right lung

left lung

left atrium

right atrium

left ventricle

right ventricle

capillaries

Oxygen-rich blood exchanges oxygen for carbon dioxide in the capillaries.

# Heart contractions

Heart contractions occur in a set pattern. This pattern is controlled by a group of cells at the top of the heart called the heart pacemaker. This makes the heart beat regularly and keeps blood moving through the system. The contractions push the blood from the atria into the ventricles and then out through the arteries. The valves open to allow blood to flow through the chambers and close to stop blood flowing in the wrong direction.

### FASCINATING FACT
Normal heart rates differ between animals. The slowest heart rate, which is just a few beats per minute, is found in hibernating mammals. The hummingbird has the fastest heart rate of 2,000 beats per minute.

First the two atria contract and then the two ventricles contract.

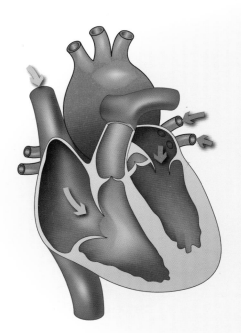

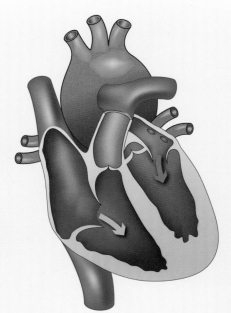

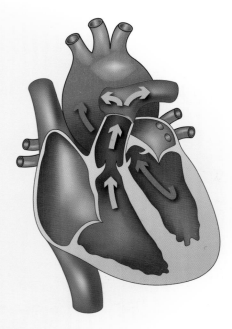

Blood fills the atria.

The atria contract, pushing blood into the ventricles.

The ventricles contract, pushing blood out of the heart.

# The function of blood

The main function of blood is to transport oxygen, nutrients, and wastes around the body. Blood also defends the body against disease, and clots to close off wounds. Different parts of the blood have different functions.

## Plasma

Plasma carries nutrients such as sugars, fats, proteins, vitamins, and minerals to the body tissues. It also contains substances that help close off wounds and carries chemical messengers called hormones.

## Red blood cells

Red blood cells, or erythrocytes (say e-rith-ro-sites), carry oxygen and carbon dioxide around the body. It is the hemoglobin in the red blood cells that carries these gases.

## White blood cells

White blood cells, or leucocytes (say loo-ko-sites), protect against disease.

## Platelets

Platelets prevent fluid leaking from wounds. They do this by sticking to areas of a wound and releasing a substance that triggers blood clotting.

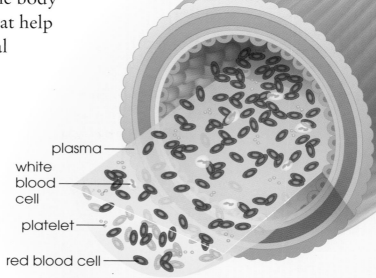

plasma
white blood cell
platelet
red blood cell

Blood cells are transported around the body in plasma.

**FASCINATING FACT**
Blood stops flowing from small wounds in around one minute and clots in about three minutes.

# Changes in the circulatory system

As humans grow, their heart rate decreases and the volume of blood in the body increases. There are many changes in the circulation through life, but the most dramatic is at birth.

## Before birth

Though a baby's heart beats before birth, it does not function as part of the circulatory system until after birth. Before birth, a baby gets its food and oxygen from its mother's body through an organ called the placenta. An unborn baby's heart has an opening, or hole, between the left and right atria called the foramen ovale. The foramen ovale stops the blood being pumped to the lungs by directing it straight into the left atrium.

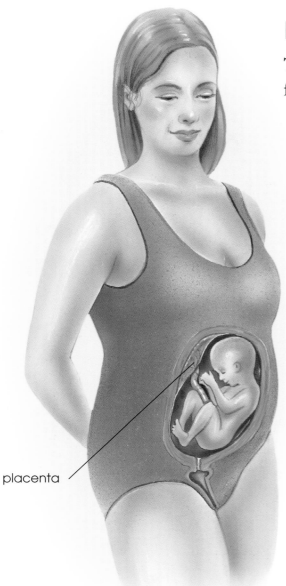

placenta

### FASCINATING FACT
A baby's developing heart can be affected by a disease the mother is carrying. Uncontrolled diabetes and rubella can both cause problems with a developing heart.

Oxygen and other nutrients are supplied to the unborn baby through the placenta.

## At birth

Many changes happen very quickly at birth. When the baby begins to breathe, the lungs begin to function for the first time. To allow blood to flow to the lungs, pressure in the left side of the heart increases and shuts off the foramen ovale. This allows the heart and lungs to function together to bring oxygen to the blood.

## As a baby grows

As a baby's body gets bigger the volume of blood increases and the heart rate slows. A baby has only 2.1 pints (1 l) of blood, but this increases to 10.6 pints (5 l) by adulthood. A newborn baby's heart rate is about 120 beats per minute, but this slows down to an average of 72 beats per minute by adulthood.

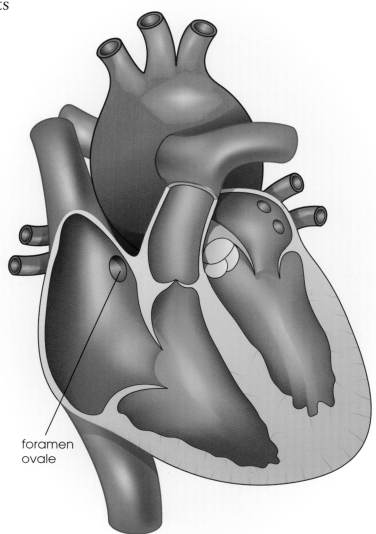

foramen
ovale

The foramen ovale, which allows blood to flow straight into the left atrium, closes at birth.

### FASCINATING FACT
Sometimes children are born with heart murmurs. The term "murmur" refers to the sounds made by the blood flowing past defective heart valves.

# Blood pressure

A person's blood pressure changes as they grow. Blood pressure is measured using a machine called a sphygmomanometer (say sfig-mo-man-om-eter). Two readings are taken when blood pressure is measured: a higher pressure and a lower pressure. The higher reading (systolic pressure) is taken when the ventricles have just contracted. The lower pressure (diastolic pressure) is taken when the ventricles are relaxed. Normal resting blood pressure for a young person is about 110/75mmHg (say 110 over 75 millimetres of mercury). Blood pressure often increases with age, but this can be minimized by eating well, exercising, and reducing stress.

## TRY THIS

### Find your own pulse

You can feel your pulse at the radial artery in your wrist, at the popliteal artery behind your knee, at the femoral artery in your groin, at the brachial artery inside your elbow, and at the carotid artery in your neck.

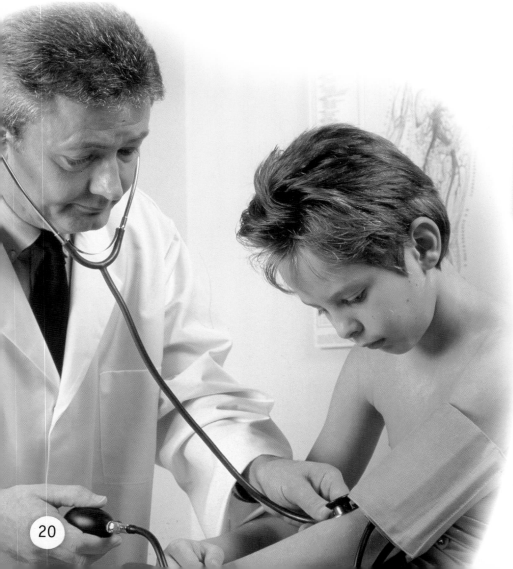

Blood pressure is usually measured in the upper arm.

## Heart rate variations

The heart rate varies with different activities according to the amount of oxygen needed by the body's tissues. When demand for oxygen increases, the heart beats faster to deliver more oxygen to the tissues. Most people have a resting heart rate of about 60 to 80 beats per minute (72 is average for adults). During exercise an adult's heart rate can go up to 200 beats per minute. Above that level the human heart is said to become incompetent; it is beating so fast that blood can no longer be pushed out with each beat.

## Changes to resting heart rate

The resting heart rate decreases as the heart grows larger. Babies have a small heart that must beat faster to pump enough blood around the body. As a child's heart grows, the amount of blood it can pump out with each beat increases, and the heart rate decreases.

!

### FASCINATING FACT
Humans have a slow heart rate compared with mice, which have a heart rate of more than 500 beats per minute. Elephants have a resting heart rate of around 20 to 30 beats per minute.

Count the number of beats in 15 seconds and multiply by four to give the heart rate in beats per minute.

# Keeping the circulatory system healthy

Keeping your body healthy will help to keep your circulatory system in good health. Many circulatory system problems can be avoided by maintaining a healthy lifestyle.

## Diet and the heart

Food is an important factor in keeping the circulatory system healthy. A balance of nutrients is required in a person's daily diet. Too much fat, especially animal fats, can cause clogging of blood vessels which may lead to heart disease. Diets high in salt have also been linked to high blood pressure.

### HEALTH TIP
#### Iron in blood

Hemoglobin molecules are built around iron. Iron-rich food is necessary for maintaining red blood cell numbers.

**Tip: Eat a serving of iron-rich food, such as red meat, beans, or wholemeal bread each day.**

People of all ages need to eat a balanced diet to keep their circulatory system healthy.

# Exercise for the heart

Regular exercise, along with eating the right foods, can help keep the heart muscle strong and circulation flowing smoothly. Activities such as running or swimming require muscles to use more oxygen which makes the heart beat harder and faster. This type of exercise, called **aerobic exercise**, increases breathing and heart rates. This workout helps make the heart muscle stronger.

## How much exercise?

To stay healthy, it is suggested that adults get a total of at least 20 minutes per day of moderate exercise several days a week. Moderate exercise should increase the heart rate to the target heart rate, which is calculated on a person's maximum heart rate. The target heart rate varies from one person to the next and depends on a person's age and level of fitness.

## Target heart rates

The table below shows the average target heart rates for ordinary, healthy people.

| Age group | Target heart rate during exercise |
|---|---|
| Children aged 10 years | 170 |
| Teenagers and young adults | 165 |
| Mature adults | 105 |

**TRY THIS**

### Are you active enough?

Some experts suggest that 20 minutes of aerobic exercise per day is too little if you are inactive most days.

Keep a record of how much exercise you get in a week.

#### Monday

| Activity | Duration |
|---|---|
| Walking to school | 15 minutes |
| Running at lunchtime | 5 minutes |
| Soccer training | 90 minutes |

# Circulatory problems

The heart, blood vessels, and blood can all suffer from disease.

## High blood pressure

Ongoing high blood pressure is called hypertension. Hypertension is associated with poor diet and lack of exercise. This condition increases the risk of circulatory disorders such as **stroke** and heart attack.

### HEALTH TIP
**Heart health**

Eating fish oils seems to protect the heart and circulation. Diets that are low in salt and fat are recommended, especially for people with high blood pressure.

*Tip: Eat fish each week for a healthy diet.*

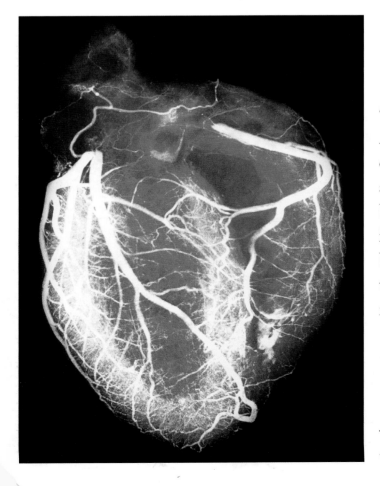

## Angina

Angina is a strong gripping pain in the chest which often extends down the left arm or to the jaw. A pain in the chest may be a warning sign that the heart muscle is not getting enough blood. Narrowed blood vessels can be widened using drugs that allow more blood to get to the heart muscle.

This angiogram shows the coronary arteries, which can become narrow and cause angina.

# Heart attack

A heart attack is when blood supply to the heart muscle is blocked in the coronary arteries, causing the heart muscle to die. Heart attack usually occurs suddenly and with little warning. The main symptom of heart attack is intense pain in the chest or down the left arm. If the heart stops during a heart attack it is called a cardiac arrest, and may lead to death if medical assistance is not provided quickly.

## Major circulatory problems

Circulatory problems can be caused by a range of contributing factors.

| Disease | Structures affected | Symptoms | Contributing factors |
|---|---|---|---|
| hypertension | blood vessels | stroke or heart failure | smoking, lack of exercise, being overweight, high blood pressure, diabetes |
| coronary heart disease | coronary arteries | chest pain (angina), heart attack | smoking, lack of exercise, being overweight, high blood pressure, diabetes |
| heart rhythm disorders | nerves controlling heart beats | irregular heart rhythm (arrhythmia) | coronary heart disease, abnormal heart development |
| cardiomyopathy | heart muscle | tiredness, lack of energy, chest pain | caused by a virus in the heart |
| heart failure | heart muscle | coughing, fatigue, swelling in the body | coronary heart disease |
| thrombosis | blood vessels | blood clots, pain and loss of function in the affected area | diet high in fat or salt, stress |
| anaemia | red blood cells | tiredness | lack of iron in diet |
| leukaemia | white blood cells | low resistance to infection, tiredness | **genetic factors**, cancer causing chemicals |

# Diagnosing problems

Modern medical imaging and surgical techniques have led to much better diagnosis and treatment of heart and circulation problems. Medical research continues to help scientists develop greater understanding of circulatory diseases.

## Images of the heart

A wide range of treatments rely on doctors being able to see into the heart before and during operations. Small cameras are used to allow doctors to perform some heart surgery procedures without cutting the chest open.

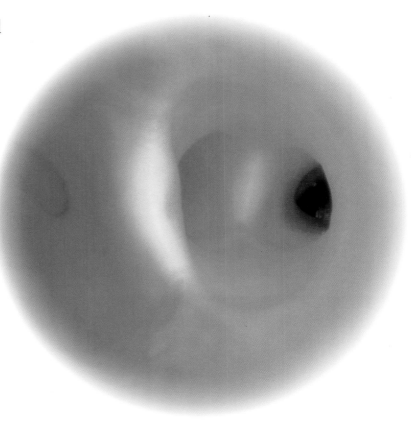

This photo of the inside of a healthy artery was taken using a small camera in a flexible tube.

## Bypass surgery

Sometimes the main coronary artery is so damaged it must be replaced, usually with a small vein from the leg. This is done in an operation where the action of the heart must be stopped. A heart lung machine is used to pump blood around the body and transfer oxygen into the blood and carbon dioxide out of the blood.

### TRY THIS

Become an organ donor

Some diseases can be treated with a heart transplant operation, using a heart from an organ donor. Organ donors are people who have elected to donate their organs if they die in an accident. Children can register if they are willing to be an organ donor.

# Blood diseases

Blood diseases can be diagnosed by analyzing blood samples.

## Anemia

Anemia (say a-nee-mee-a) is a lack of red blood cells, or when red blood cells have a reduced ability to carry oxygen.

## Leukemia

Leukemia (say loo-kee-mee-a) is a set of white blood cell disorders. The number of white blood cells in the bone marrow increases and crowds out other cells. Some forms of leukemia are common in children. They can be treated with radiation therapy and bone marrow transplants.

## Clotting disorders

In diseases such as hemophilia (say hee-ma-fil-ee-a), blood does not clot properly. Bleeding from simple cuts can be life-threatening if it cannot be stopped. Treatment may include blood transfusions, or transferring blood from a blood bank.

**FASCINATING FACT**
Scurvy, a bleeding disorder, was common in the days of long sea voyages. Travelers lacked vitamin C in their diet, which caused spontaneous bleeding and eventually death. British sailors become known as "limey" because they ate limes to prevent scurvy.

This smear of blood from a leukemia patient shows a higher than normal number of white blood cells (purple).

# Safety and first aid

When you get a small cut, the bleeding soon stops and a blood clot appears. After the wound is cleaned, it heals itself in around a week.

A scab protects a wound while it heals.

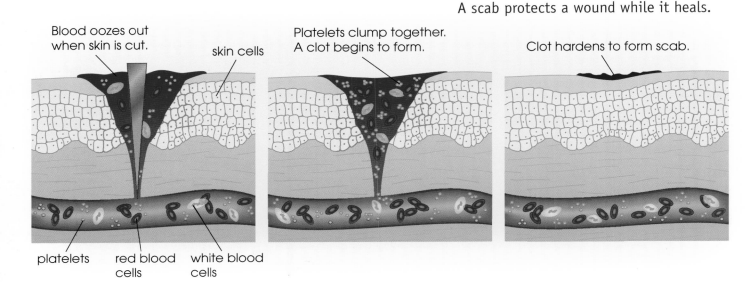

Blood oozes out when skin is cut.

skin cells

Platelets clump together. A clot begins to form.

Clot hardens to form scab.

platelets    red blood cells    white blood cells

## Major injury

A serious wound, such as a large cut with a sharp knife, may cause a large loss of blood. The wound must be held closed until it is treated by a doctor.

Apply pressure to the wound to stop the blood flow while you seek help. Large cuts are stitched together to keep the wound closed while it heals.

## Cleaning and infections

If wounds are not cleaned properly they can become infected. Bleeding helps clean a wound, as germs flow out with the blood. Warm salty water is an effective way to clean small wounds. Cutting yourself on rusty metal or wire can cause a disease called **tetanus**, so a tetanus injection may be necessary.

## Taking care of circulation

Getting enough exercise and having a good diet is essential for good circulation. Regular aerobic exercise significantly reduces risk factors for circulatory diseases.

## In case of emergency

It is not always obvious when someone has had a heart attack. Sometimes they just feel a little sick in the stomach and dizzy. Recovery is greatly increased by getting immediate medical attention. If you are nearby when someone suffers severe chest pain, it is important to know what to do. You should:

• stay calm
• ask the sufferer where it hurts and what sort of pain they are feeling
• seek medical advice.

## Be prepared

Learn emergency service numbers and practice what to ask for (police, ambulance, or fire services) in the event of an emergency. In the United States emergency services are contacted by dialling 911.

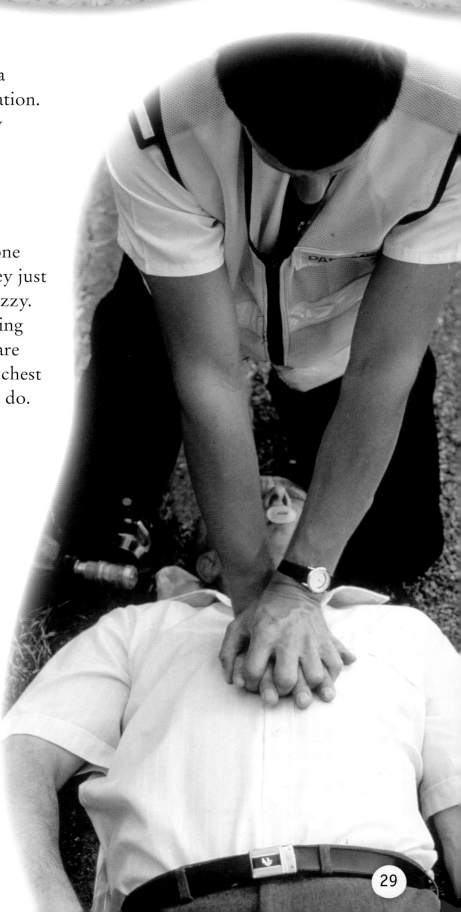

Heart massage is a first aid treatment for a person whose heart has stopped beating.

# ACTIVITY Make a stethoscope

Doctors use an instrument called a stethoscope to listen to the heart beat. You can make your own stethoscope using some everyday items.

## You will need

- a small plastic funnel
- three-way hose connector
- about 3 feet (1 m) of plastic tubing

## What to do

1 Cut the tubing into three even pieces (each about 12 inches).

2 Connect one end of each piece of tubing to the three-way connector.

3 Connect the funnel to the other end of one of the tubes.

## Using the stethoscope

Hold the two open tubes close to your ears (do not put them too far into your ears) and ask a friend to hold the funnel on their chest. Listen for two parts of the heart beat, a "lub dup" sound.

# Glossary

| | |
|---|---|
| **aerobic exercise** | exercise which increases breathing and heart rates |
| **arteries** | large blood vessels which carry blood away from the heart |
| **atria** | the upper chambers of the heart (a single chamber is an atrium) |
| **blood vessels** | tubes that carry blood through the body |
| **bone marrow** | Jell-O-like material that is found inside some bones |
| **capillaries** | the smallest blood vessels, which have thin walls |
| **carbon dioxide** | a waste gas that is produced in the tissues and removed through the lungs |
| **cells** | the smallest units of living things |
| **clot** | when blood forms a solid lump |
| **coronary arteries** | the blood vessels that supply blood to the heart muscle |
| **coronary veins** | the blood vessels that carry blood away from the heart muscle |
| **genetic factors** | inherited, or passed on in a family from one generation to the next |
| **hemoglobin** | the part of red blood cells that carries oxygen |
| **molecules** | the smallest units of a substance |
| **oxygen** | gas that humans breathe in and use for fuel |
| **plasma** | the liquid part of blood which is colorless |
| **pulse** | the rhythmic expansion and relaxation of arteries as blood is pumped through them by the heart |
| **stroke** | a disruption to the blood supply to the brain, which damages the brain |
| **tetanus** | a disease caused by bacteria which enters the body through wounds |
| **tissues** | groups of similar cells which make up the fabric of body systems |
| **veins** | blood vessels which carry blood to the heart |
| **ventricles** | the lower chambers of the heart |
| **wastes** | unwanted products produced by the body |

# Index